Influencer Impact: Smart TikTok Marketing Strategies for Success

Chapter 1: Understanding TikTok as a Marketing Platform

The Rise of TikTok

The Rise of TikTok has reshaped the landscape of social media, carving out a unique space for short-form video content that resonates with diverse audiences. Launched in 2016, TikTok quickly gained traction, particularly among younger users who were drawn to its engaging format and creative possibilities. The app's algorithm, which tailors content to individual preferences, has allowed videos to go viral with remarkable speed, making it an attractive platform for influencers and brands alike. This unprecedented growth has not only transformed how users consume content but also how businesses approach marketing strategies in the digital age.

One of the key factors contributing to TikTok's rapid ascendance is its emphasis on creativity and user-generated content. The platform encourages users to express themselves through a variety of formats, including dance challenges, lip-syncing, and comedic skits. This has led to the emergence of viral trends that capture the collective imagination, often transcending age and demographic boundaries. As small businesses recognize the power of these trends, they are increasingly leveraging TikTok's unique features to engage with potential customers, drive brand awareness, and foster community connections.

For influencers, TikTok presents a plethora of opportunities to cultivate a personal brand while experimenting with innovative marketing strategies. The platform's focus on authenticity and relatability allows influencers to build genuine connections with their followers, leading to higher engagement rates compared to other social media channels. By utilizing TikTok's tools, such as effects, filters, and sound bites, influencers can create compelling content that not only entertains but also informs their audience about products and services, paving the way for monetization through sponsorships and affiliate marketing.

Moreover, the analytics capabilities provided by TikTok empower users to track performance and refine their content strategies effectively. Understanding metrics such as views, likes, shares, and audience demographics enables creators to tailor their approach, ensuring their content resonates with the target audience. By harnessing these insights, both influencers and small businesses can optimize their presence on the platform, ultimately leading to sustainable growth and increased visibility.

As TikTok continues to evolve, the collaborative nature of the platform fosters networking opportunities among creators and brands. By participating in challenges, duets, and collaborations, users can expand their reach and attract new followers. This sense of community not only enhances the platform's appeal but also supports the growth of diverse niches. As the rise of TikTok reshapes the influencer marketing landscape, understanding and adapting to these dynamics will be crucial for anyone looking to succeed in this vibrant and rapidly changing environment.

How TikTok Differs from Other Social Media Platforms

TikTok stands out among social media platforms due to its unique focus on short-form video content that encourages creativity and spontaneity. Unlike platforms that prioritize text or image-based posts, TikTok immerses users in a dynamic audiovisual experience, enabling them to express ideas in a fast-paced and engaging manner. The platform's algorithm promotes content based on user interaction rather than follower count, allowing even new creators to gain visibility and potentially go viral with compelling content. This democratization of content discovery reshapes how brands and influencers approach their strategies on the platform.

Another key difference lies in TikTok's emphasis on trends and challenges. While other social media platforms may also feature trending topics, TikTok's format encourages users to participate actively through dance challenges, lip-syncing, and creative remixes. This participatory culture fosters a sense of community and collaboration, as users often build on each other's ideas. For small businesses and influencers, tapping into these trends can lead to increased engagement and broader reach, as users are more likely to share and interact with content that aligns with current viral themes.

TikTok's editing tools and effects further differentiate it from other platforms. The app provides a range of features, including filters, music overlays, and special effects, designed to enhance storytelling and creativity. This accessibility allows users to produce high-quality content without the need for professional editing software. For content creators and marketers, mastering these tools is essential to creating eye-catching videos that resonate with their audience. This capability not only enhances the entertainment value of posts but also supports businesses in crafting memorable brand narratives.

In terms of audience engagement, TikTok fosters a unique environment where interactions are often more immediate and personal. The platform's design encourages comments, shares, and duets, creating a two-way dialogue between creators and their followers. This immediate feedback loop is less prevalent on platforms like Facebook or Instagram, where interactions can feel more transactional. For influencers and small businesses, this means that building relationships with their audience can lead to higher levels of trust and loyalty, essential factors for long-term success.

Finally, TikTok's approach to monetization is distinct from other social media networks. While platforms like Instagram have established pathways for sponsorships and affiliate marketing, TikTok is still evolving its monetization strategies. The platform offers creators options like the TikTok Creator Fund and brand partnerships, but the focus remains on organic engagement and creativity. This dynamic requires influencers and brands to be innovative in their marketing strategies, leveraging TikTok's unique features to cultivate a loyal following and explore new revenue streams. Understanding these differences is crucial for anyone looking to succeed in the fast-paced world of TikTok marketing.

The Importance of TikTok in Modern Marketing

The rise of TikTok has transformed the landscape of modern marketing, offering unprecedented opportunities for brands and influencers to connect with audiences in innovative and engaging ways. With over a billion active users worldwide, TikTok has positioned itself as a dominant platform for content creation and consumption. Its algorithm favors creativity and authenticity, enabling even small businesses to gain visibility and reach potential customers effectively. As brands increasingly recognize the platform's unique power, understanding its role in marketing strategies becomes essential for success.

TikTok's emphasis on short, engaging videos allows marketers to convey messages quickly and creatively. This format caters to the decreasing attention spans of consumers, making it easier to capture their interest within seconds. The platform's viral nature means that content can spread rapidly, providing opportunities for small businesses to gain traction without substantial advertising budgets. By leveraging trends, challenges, and user-generated content, brands can create relatable and shareable material that resonates with their target audience.

Engaging storytelling techniques are crucial for standing out in the crowded TikTok space. Marketers can utilize narrative arcs that resonate with viewers, making their content feel personal and relatable. This approach fosters a deeper connection between the brand and the audience, encouraging them to engage with the content and share it within their networks. By focusing on authentic storytelling, brands can differentiate themselves from competitors and build a loyal following, which is vital for long-term success on the platform.

Analytics and performance tracking play a significant role in optimizing TikTok marketing strategies. Understanding metrics such as views, likes, shares, and audience demographics allows brands and influencers to refine their content and target their efforts more effectively. By analyzing which types of content perform best, marketers can adapt their strategies to align with audience preferences, ultimately driving engagement and conversions. This data-driven approach ensures that marketing efforts are not only creative but also strategic and results-oriented.

Collaboration and networking are fundamental aspects of TikTok marketing that can amplify reach and impact. By partnering with other creators or brands, influencers can tap into new audiences and enhance their visibility. Collaborations often lead to innovative content ideas that leverage the strengths of both parties, resulting in more engaging and diverse material. Additionally, exploring monetization avenues such as sponsorships and affiliate marketing can provide financial incentives for creators, further motivating them to produce high-quality content. In this dynamic ecosystem, the importance of TikTok in modern marketing cannot be overstated, as it continues to reshape how brands interact with consumers.

Chapter 2: Succeeding on TikTok

Defining Your Goals and Audience

Defining your goals and audience is a crucial first step in crafting a successful TikTok marketing strategy. Whether you are a small business owner, an aspiring influencer, or a content creator looking to capitalize on viral trends, understanding your objectives will shape every aspect of your TikTok presence. Goals can range from increasing brand awareness and driving sales to building a community or simply gaining followers. Each goal requires a tailored approach to content creation and audience engagement, ensuring that your efforts are aligned with your desired outcomes.

Identifying your target audience is equally important. TikTok is a diverse platform with a wide array of users, each with unique preferences and interests. To effectively reach and engage with your audience, you must define who they are. Consider factors such as age, location, interests, and behaviors. Conducting research through TikTok analytics or by observing successful creators in your niche can provide valuable insights. Knowing your audience helps in crafting content that resonates, leading to higher engagement rates and more impactful interactions.

Once you have your goals and audience defined, you can develop a content strategy that is both coherent and engaging. For instance, if your goal is to promote a small business, your content should focus on showcasing your products or services in a relatable way. This could involve participating in viral dance challenges while incorporating your brand in a fun context. Alternatively, if you aim to become an influencer, your focus might shift towards storytelling techniques that connect with your audience on a personal level, building trust and authenticity.

In addition to content creation, tracking your performance through TikTok analytics is essential for understanding the effectiveness of your strategies. Monitoring key metrics such as views, likes, shares, and comments will help you assess whether you are meeting your goals. This data can inform future content decisions, allowing you to pivot when necessary. If a particular trend or format resonates well with your audience, you can double down on those strategies to maximize your reach and engagement.

Finally, always be open to collaboration and networking within the TikTok community. Building relationships with other creators can amplify your reach and introduce your content to new audiences. Collaborations can also inspire fresh ideas and techniques that enhance your content. By continuously defining and refining your goals and understanding your audience, you position yourself for sustained success on TikTok, whether through viral content, effective marketing strategies, or personal branding efforts.

Developing a Unique Voice and Style

Developing a unique voice and style is essential for standing out on TikTok, where millions of creators compete for attention. This individuality not only captures viewers' interest but also fosters a sense of connection and authenticity. To cultivate a distinct voice, creators should first reflect on their personal experiences, values, and passions. By sharing stories that resonate with their audience, they can establish a relatable persona that encourages engagement and builds a loyal following. Understanding one's audience is crucial; knowing what resonates with them allows creators to tailor their content effectively.

In the realm of TikTok, visual and auditory elements play a significant role in shaping a creator's style. The choice of colors, music, and editing techniques can enhance the overall aesthetic and feel of the videos. Small businesses and influencers should experiment with different styles to find what best represents their brand while appealing to their target audience. For example, a vibrant, upbeat style may work well for dance challenges, while a more subdued, informative tone might be better suited for educational content. Consistency in these elements helps reinforce a creator's identity, making it easier for viewers to recognize their content amidst a sea of videos.

Storytelling is a powerful tool in developing a unique voice on TikTok. Engaging narratives can transform ordinary content into captivating experiences that keep viewers coming back for more. Creators should focus on crafting stories that reflect their personal journeys, struggles, and successes, allowing their audience to connect on a deeper level. Additionally, utilizing popular trends in storytelling can enhance relatability, as viewers often engage more with content that reflects their own experiences. Whether it's humor, inspiration, or vulnerability, infusing personal stories into videos can significantly boost audience engagement.

Analyzing successful TikTok creators can provide valuable insights into developing a unique voice. By studying how others express their individuality, creators can identify effective techniques that resonate with their audiences. This analysis should not be about imitation but rather adaptation; understanding what works for others can inspire new ideas and approaches. Furthermore, staying updated with current trends and shifts in audience preferences ensures that a creator's voice evolves over time, remaining fresh and relevant in the ever-changing TikTok landscape.

Finally, networking and collaboration with other creators can enhance the development of a unique voice and style. Partnering with influencers who share similar values or target audiences can introduce creators to new perspectives and techniques. These collaborations can lead to innovative content that combines different styles and voices, enriching the overall TikTok experience. By actively engaging with the TikTok community through comments, duets, and challenges, creators not only refine their style but also expand their reach, fostering a collaborative environment that benefits all involved.

Best Practices for Posting Frequency and Timing

Posting frequency and timing are critical components of a successful TikTok strategy. Finding the right balance between how often you post and when can significantly impact your engagement levels and overall reach. Generally, it is recommended to post consistently, whether that means daily, several times a week, or weekly, depending on your content capacity and audience preferences. Regular posting keeps your audience engaged and increases the chances of your videos being seen by a broader audience. Consistency fosters familiarity, which can lead to increased follower loyalty and interaction over time.

Understanding your audience is essential when determining the best times to post. Each TikTok account has a unique audience, and their active hours can vary. Utilizing TikTok Analytics is a valuable tool for identifying when your followers are most active. By reviewing your analytics, you can pinpoint the optimal times to share your content, ensuring that your posts reach the largest possible audience. Experimenting with different posting times can also help you identify patterns in engagement, allowing you to refine your strategy further.

In addition to timing, adjusting your posting frequency based on content type and trends is crucial. For instance, viral trends or challenges often require timely participation to maximize visibility and engagement. In these cases, increasing your posting frequency temporarily can help you capitalize on the moment. However, quality should never be sacrificed for quantity. It's important to ensure that every post adds value to your audience, whether through entertainment, information, or inspiration. This balance will help maintain your brand integrity while still engaging effectively with trends.

Engaging storytelling techniques can also influence your posting strategy. Videos that tell a story or convey a message are more likely to resonate with viewers, encouraging them to share your content. Crafting a narrative can make your posts more memorable and impactful. By focusing on storytelling, you can create a series of connected posts, leading to increased frequency without compromising quality. Consider planning a content calendar that allows for both standalone posts and series that build upon one another, engaging viewers over time.

Lastly, collaborating with other creators can enhance your posting frequency and timing strategies. Partnerships can introduce your content to new audiences and offer fresh perspectives. Collaborating with others can also allow for shared content creation, making it easier to maintain a consistent posting schedule. When planning collaborations, consider aligning your posting times to maximize the impact of your joint efforts. By leveraging each other's audiences and expertise, you can create a more dynamic presence on TikTok, leading to greater growth and engagement.

Chapter 3: TikTok Content Creation for Small Businesses

Identifying Your Brand's Niche

Identifying your brand's niche on TikTok is a crucial step in establishing a successful presence on the platform. With its diverse user base and a wide array of content types, TikTok presents both opportunities and challenges for brands and influencers aiming to stand out. To carve out a unique space, it is essential to understand what sets your brand apart and how it aligns with the interests and preferences of your target audience. This involves researching current trends, identifying gaps in the market, and defining your unique selling proposition (USP).

Start by analyzing the content that resonates with viewers within your desired niche. For instance, if your focus is on TikTok content creation for small businesses, observe how successful accounts engage their audiences. Pay attention to the types of videos that garner high engagement, such as tutorials, behind-the-scenes looks, or customer testimonials. This analysis not only helps in understanding what works but also aids in refining your content strategy to meet the expectations of your audience while staying true to your brand identity.

Viral dance challenges and trends are another area where niche identification plays a significant role. Participating in these challenges can propel your visibility, but it's important to choose trends that align with your brand values and target audience. For example, a fitness brand might leverage dance challenges by incorporating workout routines into their videos, creating a seamless connection between the trend and their core message. This strategic approach ensures that your content is not only entertaining but also relevant, enhancing your brand's authenticity and appeal.

Engaging storytelling techniques are essential in making your brand's niche more compelling.

Crafting narratives that resonate emotionally with viewers can help deepen their connection to your brand. Whether you are sharing personal anecdotes, customer success stories, or even humorous skits, the key is to maintain a consistent voice and theme throughout your content. Effective storytelling can differentiate your brand and foster loyalty among viewers who relate to your message, ultimately contributing to your brand's growth and recognition on TikTok.

Lastly, leveraging TikTok analytics and performance tracking tools can provide valuable insights into how well your niche-focused content is performing. By regularly monitoring metrics such as viewer engagement, watch time, and follower growth, you can make informed decisions about your content strategy. This data-driven approach allows you to refine your tactics, experiment with new ideas, and adapt to the ever-changing landscape of TikTok, ensuring that your brand remains relevant and continues to thrive within your chosen niche.

Crafting Engaging Content Ideas

Crafting engaging content ideas is essential for anyone looking to thrive on TikTok, whether you are an aspiring influencer, a small business owner, or simply someone keen on sharing creative videos. The platform's unique algorithm rewards creativity and originality, making it crucial to brainstorm and refine ideas that resonate with your target audience. Engaging content often starts with understanding current trends and audience preferences, which can be achieved by regularly browsing TikTok, participating in popular challenges, and analyzing the success of other creators.

One effective approach to generating content ideas is to tap into trending topics and challenges. Regularly monitoring the "For You" page will help you identify what's currently popular, allowing you to create timely and relevant videos. By participating in viral dance challenges or trends, you can leverage the existing excitement and visibility to attract viewers. Additionally, consider adding your unique spin to these trends, whether through humor, storytelling, or showcasing a personal experience, to stand out from the crowd and encourage viewer engagement.

Another strategy for crafting engaging content is to focus on storytelling. TikTok thrives on authentic narratives, so consider how you can weave your message into a compelling story. This could be a behind-the-scenes look at your business, a personal anecdote related to a challenge you're facing, or a humorous take on everyday situations. By connecting with your audience emotionally, you can foster a sense of relatability and community, which is vital for building a loyal following on the platform.

Utilizing analytics tools is also key to refining your content ideas. By analyzing the performance of your past videos, you can identify which themes and formats resonate most with your audience. Pay attention to metrics such as watch time, likes, shares, and comments to understand what captivates your viewers. This data-driven approach not only helps in crafting future content but also enables you to adapt your strategies based on audience feedback, ensuring that you remain relevant in a fast-paced environment.

Finally, collaboration can open doors to new content ideas. Partnering with other TikTok creators or influencers can introduce your brand to their audience while providing fresh perspectives on content creation. Whether it's through joint challenges, shoutouts, or co-hosted live sessions, these collaborations can enhance your visibility and inspire innovative content ideas. Engaging with others in your niche can lead to fruitful exchanges of ideas, resulting in videos that captivate and entertain a broader audience. By combining these strategies, you can consistently develop engaging content that resonates with viewers and supports your goals on TikTok.

Utilizing User-Generated Content

User-generated content (UGC) has emerged as a powerful tool for TikTok marketers and influencers alike. This content, created by users rather than brands, offers authenticity and relatability that can significantly enhance engagement. By harnessing the creativity and enthusiasm of your audience, you can amplify your brand message, foster community, and drive organic growth. UGC can take many forms, including videos, comments, challenges, and duets, each providing a unique opportunity to connect with viewers on a personal level.

One effective strategy for utilizing UGC is to encourage your followers to participate in challenges or trends that align with your brand. By creating a branded hashtag and inviting users to share their own interpretations, you can generate a wealth of content that not only promotes your brand but also showcases the creativity of your audience. This strategy not only boosts visibility but also fosters a sense of community among your followers, as they see others engaging with the same challenge and brand. As this content circulates, it can attract new followers who are drawn to the vibrant community you've cultivated.

Additionally, engaging with UGC can enhance your brand's credibility. When potential customers see real people using and enjoying your products or services, it builds trust and authenticity. Sharing UGC on your own profile showcases your appreciation for your followers while providing social proof that your offerings are valuable. Highlighting user-generated content in your marketing strategy helps create a two-way interaction, where followers feel valued and more likely to remain loyal to your brand.

To effectively track the impact of UGC, leverage TikTok analytics tools. These tools allow you to monitor engagement metrics on content that features user submissions. By analyzing which types of UGC resonate most with your audience, you can refine your marketing strategies and adjust your approach to better align with viewer preferences. This data-driven approach ensures that you continually engage your audience in a manner that feels relevant and exciting, ultimately driving further growth and interaction.

Lastly, building partnerships with influencers or encouraging collaborations within your community can enhance the reach of your UGC efforts. By working with creators who align with your brand values, you can tap into their audience while simultaneously encouraging their followers to engage with your brand. This collaboration could manifest in challenges, joint content creation, or shout-outs that motivate followers to participate and share their own experiences. Utilizing UGC not only fosters a deeper connection with your audience but also sets the foundation for a thriving and engaged community around your brand on TikTok.

Chapter 4: Viral Dance Challenges and Trends

Understanding the Mechanics of Viral Trends

Understanding the mechanics of viral trends on TikTok is essential for anyone looking to harness the platform's full potential for marketing and content creation. Viral trends often emerge from a combination of creativity, relatability, and the platform's unique algorithm, which promotes content that resonates with a wide audience. By grasping how these trends function, content creators and businesses can align their strategies to take advantage of the fleeting nature of virality, ensuring that their messages reach and engage as many people as possible.

At the core of viral trends is the concept of relatability. Users are drawn to content that reflects their own experiences, feelings, or humor. This relatability often manifests through dance challenges, memes, or sound bites that echo shared cultural moments. For small businesses and influencers, tapping into these shared experiences can enhance their visibility. By crafting content that connects with current trends, brands can create a sense of community with their audience. This connection not only boosts engagement but also encourages users to participate in the trend, further spreading the brand's reach.

The TikTok algorithm plays a crucial role in determining which content goes viral. It prioritizes engagement metrics such as likes, shares, comments, and watch time. Understanding these mechanics means that creators need to focus on producing content that not only fits within a trend but also encourages interaction. For instance, incorporating questions, calls to action, or challenges can prompt viewers to engage, increasing the likelihood of the content being shared and displayed on more "For You" pages. This strategic approach to content creation can significantly enhance the chances of achieving virality.

Another essential aspect of viral trends is the speed at which they evolve. Trends can rise and fall within days or even hours, making it imperative for content creators to stay updated on the latest happenings within the TikTok community. Engaging with other creators, monitoring trending hashtags, and actively participating in challenges can help identify and capitalize on these fleeting opportunities. Small businesses can utilize this knowledge to pivot their marketing strategies quickly, ensuring they remain relevant and in tune with their audience's interests.

Lastly, the art of storytelling cannot be overlooked when discussing viral trends. Engaging storytelling techniques can elevate content from merely being part of a trend to becoming a memorable piece that resonates with viewers. This involves crafting narratives that are not only entertaining but also convey a message or brand identity. By mastering the balance between trend participation and authentic storytelling, brands can create content that not only captures attention but also leaves a lasting impression, ultimately leading to greater brand loyalty and recognition on TikTok.

Creating Your Own Dance Challenge

Creating your own dance challenge on TikTok can be an exciting way to engage your audience and expand your reach. The first step is to develop a unique and catchy concept that resonates with your target audience. Consider the current trends and popular music on the platform, as well as the demographics of your followers. A successful dance challenge often combines a simple yet fun choreography with a relatable theme or message. This ensures that participants can easily learn the moves and feel motivated to join in.

Once you have a concept in mind, it's essential to create a signature dance routine that is easy to follow. Break down the choreography into manageable segments, making it accessible for dancers of all skill levels. Utilize clear and concise instructions, which can include video tutorials or step-by-step guides. Adding a personal touch by incorporating elements that reflect your brand or personality can also enhance the challenge's appeal. An engaging routine coupled with a relatable story can further encourage participation and sharing among users.

Promotion is key to the success of your dance challenge. Share teaser videos and behind-the-scenes content on your TikTok profile to generate excitement before the official launch. Collaborate with other influencers or TikTok creators to reach a wider audience and boost engagement. Consider using hashtags strategically to increase visibility; create a unique hashtag for your challenge that participants can use when posting their videos.

This not only helps in tracking participation but also fosters a sense of community around your challenge.

As the challenge gains traction, it's important to monitor its performance through TikTok analytics. Keep an eye on metrics such as views, likes, shares, and the number of videos created under your challenge hashtag. This data provides valuable insights into what resonates with your audience and helps you refine future content. Engaging with participants by liking, commenting, and sharing their videos can also enhance community involvement and encourage more users to join in.

Finally, consider ways to incentivize participation to further drive engagement. Offering shout-outs, featuring participants on your profile, or even running a contest with prizes can motivate users to take part in your dance challenge. By creating a fun and engaging environment, you not only promote your brand but also build a loyal community around your content. Ultimately, a well-executed dance challenge can serve as an effective marketing strategy, boosting your visibility and helping you connect with your audience on a deeper level.

Participating in Existing Trends Effectively

To participate in trends effectively, one must first monitor what is currently popular on TikTok. This involves keeping an eye on the "For You" page, using trending hashtags, and observing the type of content that is gaining traction. TikTok's algorithm favors content that aligns with current trends, which means that creators who can adapt their style or message to fit these trends are more likely to be seen. Engaging in viral dance challenges, for example, not only showcases dancing skills but also taps into a community that thrives on shared experiences. This communal aspect is essential for fostering engagement and increasing visibility.

Once a creator identifies a trend they want to participate in, it's vital to add a unique twist to their content. Simply replicating a popular video can lead to being lost in the multitude of similar posts. Instead, incorporating personal branding, a distinctive storytelling angle, or a niche-specific approach can set a creator apart. For instance, a small business could showcase how their products enhance the experience of a viral challenge, making it relevant while still adhering to the trend. This creative approach not only engages the audience but also builds a memorable connection with the brand.

Analytics play a significant role in understanding the effectiveness of participating in trends. By tracking performance metrics, creators can assess which trends resonate most with their audience and adapt future content strategies accordingly. Utilizing TikTok's built-in analytics tools allows for a clear understanding of engagement rates, viewer demographics, and the overall impact of trend participation. This data-driven approach helps refine content creation efforts, ensuring that future posts align with audience preferences and current trends.

Lastly, building a network within the TikTok community can enhance the effectiveness of participating in trends. Collaborating with other creators can introduce fresh perspectives and expand reach. By joining forces with fellow influencers or businesses that share a similar audience, creators can tap into each other's followers, thereby maximizing the impact of trend participation. Additionally, engaging with the community through comments, duets, and stitches fosters relationships that can lead to more collaborative opportunities and innovative content creation techniques.

Chapter 5: TikTok Marketing Strategies for Influencers

Building an Authentic Following

Building an authentic following on TikTok is essential for anyone looking to succeed on the platform, whether you're an individual influencer, a small business, or anyone in between. Authenticity resonates deeply with audiences, fostering trust and loyalty that can translate into higher engagement and increased visibility. The first step in building this authentic connection is to present a genuine persona that reflects your true values, interests, and passions. Audience members are quick to recognize inauthentic content, which can lead to a disengaged following. Instead, focus on showcasing your unique voice and story, allowing your audience to relate to and connect with you on a personal level.

Engaging storytelling techniques are a powerful tool for cultivating an authentic following. TikTok's format lends itself well to short, impactful narratives that grab attention within the first few seconds. Crafting stories that resonate with your audience allows them to see themselves in your content. Whether you're sharing the behind-the-scenes struggles of running a small business or the journey of mastering viral dance challenges, these narratives create a sense of community. This approach not only elevates your content but also invites followers to interact, share their own stories, and become a part of your journey.

Incorporating trends and challenges into your content can also help in establishing authenticity while staying relevant. Engaging with viral dance challenges allows you to connect with broader conversations happening on the platform. However, it's crucial to put your unique spin on these trends to maintain authenticity. Your interpretation should reflect your personal brand and resonate with your audience. This alignment between trend participation and personal branding ensures you attract followers who appreciate your originality while enjoying the trending content.

Collaboration is another key strategy for building an authentic following. Partnering with other TikTok creators or brands that share your values can not only expand your reach but also provide your audience with varied content that feels cohesive. These collaborations can take many forms, such as joint challenges, co-hosted live sessions, or even simple shout-outs. When done authentically, these partnerships can enhance your credibility and introduce you to new audiences that are likely to resonate with your content.

Lastly, leveraging TikTok analytics is crucial for understanding your audience and their preferences. Monitoring performance metrics such as engagement rates, watch times, and follower demographics can provide insights into what resonates most with your audience. By analyzing this data, you can refine your content strategy to focus on what works best, ensuring that you continue to build and maintain an authentic following. Being responsive to audience feedback and evolving your content based on analytics leads to sustained growth and a loyal community that genuinely values your contributions.

Leveraging Trends for Engagement

Leveraging trends for engagement on TikTok is essential for creators and brands looking to enhance their visibility and connect with a larger audience. Trends on TikTok can emerge rapidly, often driven by viral challenges, popular sounds, or emerging themes. To effectively leverage these trends, it is crucial to stay informed and agile. Monitoring TikTok's Discover page, engaging with trending hashtags, and following influential creators can provide insights into what content is currently resonating with users. By participating in these trends, businesses and influencers can align their content with the interests of the TikTok community, thereby improving their chances of virality and engagement.

Engagement can be significantly boosted through the strategic use of viral dance challenges. These challenges often encourage users to replicate choreography, which not only promotes user interaction but also fosters a sense of community. For small businesses, creating a unique challenge that aligns with their brand can invite user-generated content, amplifying their reach. When crafting a dance challenge, it is important to ensure that the choreography is accessible, fun, and easy to replicate. This encourages participation from a broader audience, turning a simple trend into a powerful marketing tool.

In addition to dance challenges, integrating popular sounds into content can enhance viewer engagement. TikTok's algorithm often favors videos that utilize trending audio clips, which can lead to increased visibility on users' For You pages. Brands and influencers should consider how they can creatively incorporate these sounds into their storytelling or product showcases. Whether it's through comedic skits, informative snippets, or visually captivating presentations, aligning content with trending audio can elevate its appeal and encourage viewers to engage through likes, shares, and comments.

Furthermore, understanding the analytics behind engagement metrics is vital when leveraging trends. TikTok provides various tools for performance tracking, allowing creators to analyze which trends resonate most with their audience. Metrics such as view counts, shares, and engagement rates can reveal what content is performing well and inform future strategies. By continuously monitoring these analytics, brands can refine their approach, ensuring they stay relevant and maintain engagement levels. This data-driven approach allows for smarter content creation that not only embraces current trends but also aligns with audience preferences.

Lastly, collaboration with other TikTok users can amplify engagement through the power of cross-promotion. By partnering with influencers or creators who share a similar audience or brand ethos, businesses can tap into new follower bases. Collaborations can take various forms, including duet videos, challenges, or shared storytelling. These partnerships not only enhance visibility but also create a richer content experience for viewers. By leveraging trends and collaborating effectively, brands and influencers can cultivate a vibrant TikTok presence that drives sustained engagement and growth.

Collaborating with Brands for Success

Collaborating with brands can be a game-changer for TikTok creators looking to amplify their reach and monetize their content. When influencers align with brands that resonate with their personal brand and audience, it creates a win-win situation. Brands gain access to a dedicated and engaged audience, while creators receive support, resources, and financial compensation. To maximize the benefits of these collaborations, it is essential for creators to choose partnerships that reflect their values and appeal to their followers, ensuring authenticity in every sponsored post.

Establishing a successful brand collaboration begins with clear communication. Influencers should articulate their goals, audience demographics, and engagement metrics to potential brand partners. This information helps brands understand the value that the influencer can bring to their marketing strategy. By presenting a professional image and demonstrating an understanding of the brand's objectives, influencers can position themselves as valuable assets in the eyes of brands seeking to enhance their TikTok presence.

Once a partnership is established, it's crucial to create content that seamlessly integrates the brand message with the influencer's unique style. Engaging storytelling techniques can transform a simple promotional post into an entertaining and relatable piece of content that resonates with viewers. Utilizing popular trends, creative video editing tools, and innovative formats can help in crafting compelling narratives that captivate the audience while staying true to the brand's identity. The goal should be to enhance the viewer's experience rather than interrupt it with overt advertising.

Performance tracking is another vital aspect of successful collaborations. Influencers should utilize TikTok analytics tools to monitor engagement rates, views, and audience reactions to sponsored content. This data not only provides insights into what works and what doesn't but also serves as valuable feedback for brands. By sharing these analytics with brand partners, influencers can strengthen their relationships and demonstrate their effectiveness as marketing collaborators, paving the way for future partnerships.

Finally, networking with other creators and brands can lead to even greater collaboration opportunities. Engaging with fellow influencers through comments, duets, and challenges can foster a sense of community and open doors for joint campaigns. Additionally, attending industry events and participating in online forums can help influencers connect with brand representatives. Building a robust network enhances visibility and can lead to mutually beneficial collaborations that drive growth and success for all parties involved. By strategically navigating brand partnerships, TikTok creators can significantly enhance their influence and monetization potential on the platform.

Chapter 6: Niche-Specific TikTok Growth Hacks

Identifying and Targeting Your Niche

Identifying and targeting your niche is a crucial step in maximizing your impact on TikTok. With the platform's diverse user base, pinpointing a specific audience allows creators and brands to tailor their content effectively. To begin with, understanding the unique interests and preferences of your target audience can help you create engaging content that resonates with them. Conducting thorough research on existing trends, popular content types, and the demographics of your potential followers will provide valuable insights into what niche you could excel in.

Once you have a clear understanding of your audience, it's essential to explore the various niches available on TikTok. For instance, niches such as TikTok content creation for small businesses or viral dance challenges can attract different types of viewers. Each niche has its own characteristics and audience expectations. By analyzing the content that is currently popular within these niches, you can identify gaps or opportunities where your unique voice can shine. This process not only helps in content creation but also aids in building a loyal following.

Targeting a specific niche also allows for more effective marketing strategies. Influencers and small businesses can leverage niche-specific TikTok growth hacks to accelerate their reach. By utilizing relevant hashtags, participating in challenges, and collaborating with other creators in the same niche, you can enhance your visibility and engagement rates. Moreover, understanding the nuances of TikTok analytics and performance tracking can help you refine your approach, ensuring that your content continues to meet the expectations of your audience.

Engaging storytelling techniques play a significant role in connecting with your niche. Crafting stories that reflect your brand's values or your personal experiences can create a deeper emotional connection with your viewers. This is particularly effective in niches like building a personal brand on TikTok, where authenticity is paramount. By sharing relatable narratives, you not only entertain but also inspire your audience, encouraging them to interact with your content and share it within their networks.

Lastly, monetizing your presence on TikTok is closely tied to how well you identify and target your niche. Sponsorships and affiliate marketing opportunities often arise from a well-defined audience. Brands are more likely to approach influencers who have established themselves within a specific niche, as this indicates a dedicated following that aligns with their products or services. By focusing on your niche and engaging meaningfully with your audience, you set the foundation for successful collaborations and revenue generation, transforming your TikTok presence into a thriving venture.

Utilizing Hashtags and Challenges

Hashtags and challenges are essential tools in maximizing visibility and engagement on TikTok. By strategically incorporating relevant hashtags, users can amplify their content's reach beyond their immediate followers. Hashtags categorize videos and make them discoverable to audiences who search for or follow specific themes. It's crucial to balance popular, trending hashtags with niche-specific ones to attract a targeted audience. For instance, while using a broad hashtag like #DanceChallenge may draw many viewers, adding a niche hashtag such as

#SmallBusinessDance can help connect with users interested in entrepreneurial content.

Engaging in TikTok challenges is another effective way to harness the platform's viral potential. Challenges often come with established participation rules, making it easier for users to join in and create related content. By participating in these challenges, influencers can tap into existing trends and increase their chances of being featured on the 'For You' page. This organic exposure can lead to a significant rise in followers and engagement. Small businesses can also benefit by creating their own challenges that align with their brand, encouraging user-generated content that promotes their products or services.

When utilizing hashtags and challenges, understanding TikTok's analytics tools is vital. Users should regularly track which hashtags are driving engagement and which challenges resonate with their audience. This data can inform future content strategies, allowing creators to refine their approach based on performance metrics. By analyzing views, shares, and comments, influencers and businesses can identify successful trends and replicate them, ensuring continuous growth and interaction with their content.

Storytelling techniques play a significant role when leveraging hashtags and challenges. Instead of simply participating in a trend, creators should weave their personal or brand narrative into the challenge. This unique angle makes the content more relatable and memorable, helping it stand out amidst a sea of similar videos. By creatively integrating storytelling with popular hashtags, influencers can foster a deeper connection with their audience, enhancing both engagement and retention.

Collaboration is another powerful strategy when utilizing hashtags and challenges. Partnering with other TikTok users or influencers can amplify content reach and introduce creators to new audiences. This collaborative approach can also lead to innovative content that blends different styles and ideas, making it more appealing. By leveraging each other's follower bases through shared challenges or hashtag campaigns, both parties can experience mutual growth, showcasing the power of community in TikTok marketing.

Engaging with Your Niche Community

Engaging with your niche community on TikTok is crucial for building a strong presence and fostering a loyal following. Understanding the unique interests and preferences of your target audience allows you to create content that resonates deeply with them. By actively participating in discussions, responding to comments, and sharing user-generated content, you can establish a rapport that encourages community members to engage with your brand. This interaction not only increases your visibility on the platform but also positions you as a relatable figure within your niche.

One effective strategy for engaging with your niche community is to leverage trending challenges and hashtags that align with your content. By participating in viral dance challenges or popular trends, you not only showcase your creativity but also tap into existing conversations that are capturing the attention of users. This tactic can boost your reach and connect you with like-minded individuals who share your interests. Additionally, you can create your own challenges that encourage user participation, fostering a sense of belonging among your followers.

Utilizing TikTok's features, such as duets and stitches, can further enhance your engagement with the community. These tools allow you to collaborate with other creators, showcasing their content while providing your audience with fresh perspectives. By engaging in collaborative efforts, you not only expand your reach but also add value to your niche community by highlighting diverse voices and ideas. This practice can lead to cross-promotion, where both creators benefit from each other's audiences.

Storytelling is another powerful way to connect with your niche community. Crafting relatable narratives around your experiences, challenges, and successes can captivate your audience and encourage them to share their own stories. Engaging storytelling helps to humanize your brand, making it more approachable and relatable. Whether you are sharing insights on

TikTok marketing strategies or providing tips for video editing, weaving personal anecdotes into your content can create a deeper emotional connection with your viewers.

Finally, tracking your performance through TikTok analytics is essential for understanding how well your engagement strategies are working. By analyzing data on views, likes, comments, and shares, you can identify which content resonates most with your audience. This information allows you to refine your approach, making adjustments that enhance your community engagement efforts. Keeping a pulse on your audience's preferences will enable you to maintain relevance and continue to grow your niche community effectively.

Chapter 7: TikTok Analytics and Performance Tracking

Understanding TikTok Analytics Tools

Understanding TikTok Analytics Tools is essential for anyone looking to maximize their impact on the platform. These tools provide valuable insights into audience behavior, content performance, and engagement metrics, allowing users to make data-driven decisions. By analyzing analytics, both creators and brands can tailor their strategies to enhance visibility and interaction, ultimately leading to more effective campaigns and a stronger presence on TikTok.

The main components of TikTok analytics include video views, profile views, follower growth, and engagement rates. Each of these metrics offers a different perspective on how content is performing. Video views indicate raw popularity, while profile views show interest in the creator. Follower growth is a direct measure of how well a creator is attracting and retaining an audience, and engagement rates reveal how effectively content resonates with viewers. Understanding these metrics helps creators and businesses identify trends and adjust their content strategies accordingly.

In addition to basic metrics, TikTok provides demographic insights about followers, including age, gender, and geographic location. This information is crucial for targeted marketing efforts and helps creators understand who their audience is. By knowing their audience's preferences, creators can craft content that speaks directly to their viewers, increasing the likelihood of engagement. Businesses can also use this data to tailor their marketing strategies and ensure they are reaching the right customers with their campaigns.

TikTok analytics tools also offer insights into the performance of individual videos, allowing creators to see which types of content generate the most engagement. For example, a viral dance challenge may perform exceptionally well compared to a standard promotional video. By analyzing these results, creators can replicate successful strategies and refine less effective ones. This iterative process of content creation based on analytics fosters continuous improvement and helps users stay relevant in the fast-paced TikTok environment.

Finally, leveraging TikTok analytics tools not only enhances content creation and marketing strategies but also allows for better collaboration and networking. By sharing performance data with potential partners, creators can demonstrate their reach and engagement levels, making it easier to form valuable partnerships. Whether it's for sponsorships, collaborations, or affiliate marketing, having a strong grasp of analytics can significantly boost a creator's or brand's credibility, leading to more lucrative opportunities on the platform.

Key Metrics to Monitor

When venturing into TikTok marketing, it is essential to monitor key metrics that can provide insight into the effectiveness of your strategies. Engagement rate is one of the most significant indicators, as it reflects how well your content resonates with your audience. This metric takes into account likes, comments, shares, and saves, offering a comprehensive view of how viewers interact with your videos. A high engagement rate can signal that your content is not only reaching viewers but also prompting them to take action, which is vital for building a loyal following.

Another critical metric is video views, which indicates the reach of your content. Tracking the number of views can help you understand which types of content are gaining traction and attracting a wider audience. However, it's crucial to look beyond just the numbers. Analyzing the source of these views can reveal whether they are organic or driven by paid promotions, allowing for more strategic decision-making in future campaigns. This insight can also guide content adjustments to optimize for better visibility.

Follower growth is another metric that should not be overlooked. A steady increase in followers often reflects the growing interest in your brand or content. Monitoring this metric alongside engagement can help identify which pieces of content contribute to follower retention and growth. Additionally, understanding demographic information about your followers can inform content creation that speaks directly to your target audience, further enhancing your marketing strategy.

Completion rate is an important metric as well, particularly for video content. This percentage shows how many viewers watched your video from start to finish, providing insights into content quality and viewer engagement. A high completion rate indicates that your content is captivating enough to hold viewers' attention, which is essential for encouraging shares and increasing overall reach. If the completion rate is low, it may be necessary to reevaluate the content's length, pacing, or messaging.

Finally, tracking conversion metrics, such as clicks to your website or product purchases, is vital for monetizing your TikTok efforts. These metrics demonstrate the effectiveness of your call-to-actions and can directly correlate with your business goals. By analyzing the path viewers take from your TikTok videos to your website or online store, you can refine your approach to ensure that your content not only entertains but also drives tangible results.

Monitoring these key metrics will equip you with the insights needed to refine your TikTok marketing strategies and foster lasting success.

Adjusting Strategies Based on Data

Adjusting strategies based on data is crucial for anyone looking to succeed on TikTok, whether you are a small business, an influencer, or simply someone wanting to create engaging content. The platform provides a wealth of analytics that can inform your decisions and lead to improved engagement and growth. By closely monitoring these metrics, users can pinpoint what resonates with their audience, allowing for a more targeted approach in content creation and marketing.

One of the first steps in this process is understanding TikTok's built-in analytics tools. These tools offer insights into video performance, audience demographics, and engagement rates.

For small businesses and influencers alike, this data is invaluable. It can help identify which types of content perform best, whether it be viral dance challenges, storytelling videos, or promotional content. By consistently analyzing this data, users can fine-tune their strategies to focus on high-performing content types, maximizing their reach and effectiveness.

In addition to performance metrics, tracking audience engagement can lead to significant insights. Observing when your audience is most active can inform the best times to post content. For example, if your analytics reveal that your followers are most active in the evenings, adjusting your posting schedule accordingly can increase visibility and engagement. Similarly, understanding the demographics of your audience allows for content that speaks directly to their interests and preferences, thus enhancing the chances of virality in a trend-driven platform like TikTok.

Moreover, adapting your content strategy based on data is not a one-time effort but an ongoing process. Regularly revisiting analytics after each campaign or content series can unveil patterns that may have gone unnoticed initially. For instance, if a certain format or theme consistently yields higher engagement, it's wise to explore that avenue further. This iterative approach ensures that your TikTok strategy evolves in tandem with your audience's changing tastes, enabling sustained growth and relevance.

Lastly, collaboration and networking are also influenced by data insights. By analyzing engagement metrics, you can identify potential collaborators whose audiences align with yours. This not only broadens your reach but also adds fresh perspectives to your content. Additionally, understanding the effectiveness of past collaborations can help shape future partnerships, ensuring that your efforts are both strategic and data-driven. By continuously adjusting your strategies based on data, you can enhance your TikTok presence and drive lasting impact in a competitive landscape.

Chapter 8: Engaging Storytelling Techniques for TikTok

The Power of Storytelling in Marketing

Storytelling is a fundamental element of human communication that transcends cultures and generations. In the realm of marketing, particularly on platforms like TikTok, effective storytelling can captivate audiences, foster emotional connections, and ultimately drive engagement and conversion. Unlike traditional advertising, which often relies on direct promotions, storytelling invites viewers into a narrative, making them a part of the experience. This engagement is especially crucial on TikTok, where users are inundated with content and have limited attention spans. A compelling story can make your brand stand out, resonate with your audience, and encourage them to share your message.

One of the essential components of successful storytelling is relatability. For small businesses, this means crafting stories that reflect the values, struggles, and aspirations of their target audience. By sharing authentic experiences, whether it's a behind-the-scenes look at a product's creation or a personal anecdote about overcoming challenges, brands can humanize their message. This authenticity not only builds trust but also invites viewers to engage with the content, increasing the likelihood of shares, comments, and likes. In a space where trends change rapidly, relatable storytelling can create a lasting impression that extends beyond a single video.

In the context of viral dance challenges and trends, storytelling can also be woven into the choreography or theme of the challenge itself. For instance, a dance challenge that tells a story of friendship or resilience can encourage participants to engage on a deeper level, making the experience more meaningful. This not only boosts participation but also enhances the likelihood of the challenge going viral. Influencers can leverage this storytelling approach by incorporating personal narratives into their dance videos, creating a connection with their audience that transcends mere entertainment.

Moreover, effective storytelling on TikTok involves understanding the platform's unique features and utilizing them to enhance your narrative. Utilizing tools such as captions, soundtracks, and visual effects can elevate your storytelling, providing context and emotional depth. For instance, pairing a heartfelt story with a trending sound can evoke feelings that resonate with viewers, prompting them to engage more deeply with the content. Additionally, editing techniques can be employed to create a narrative arc, drawing viewers in and keeping them invested until the conclusion.

Ultimately, the power of storytelling in marketing on TikTok lies in its ability to create a community around your brand. By encouraging audience participation through challenges, collaborations, and user-generated content, brands can foster a sense of belonging among their followers. This community-building aspect not only enhances brand loyalty but also opens up opportunities for monetization through sponsorships and affiliate marketing. As audiences become emotionally invested in the stories being told, they are more likely to support the brands behind those narratives, transforming storytelling into a powerful tool for marketing success.

Structuring Your TikTok Stories

Structuring your TikTok stories effectively is crucial for engaging your audience and maximizing the platform's potential. TikTok, with its short-form video format, demands that content creators capture attention quickly and maintain viewer interest throughout. The key to achieving this lies in a well-defined structure that allows for clear storytelling while also catering to the unique features of the platform. Understanding the essential components of a successful TikTok story can significantly enhance your content creation efforts, whether you're a small business, an influencer, or simply someone looking to grow their personal brand.

A compelling TikTok story typically follows a three-part structure: the setup, the conflict, and the resolution. The setup serves to introduce your topic or theme, immediately grabbing the viewer's attention. It should be visually engaging and relevant to your audience. The conflict introduces a problem or challenge that resonates with viewers, making them want to see how it unfolds. Finally, the resolution provides a satisfying conclusion, offering insight, humor, or a call to action that encourages further engagement. This structure not only enhances viewer retention but also prompts sharing and interaction, which are essential for viral success.

Incorporating elements of creativity and authenticity is vital when structuring your TikTok stories. Unique storytelling techniques, such as using humor, personal anecdotes, or unexpected twists, can make your content stand out. For small businesses, weaving brand messaging into your narrative without being overly promotional can create genuine connections with your audience. Influencers can leverage their personal experiences to craft relatable stories that resonate with their followers, fostering a sense of community and loyalty. Balancing creativity with authenticity will help you build a strong personal brand while engaging your audience effectively.

Utilizing TikTok's editing features and tools can further enhance your storytelling capabilities. Experimenting with transitions, effects, and sound can bring your stories to life and make them more visually appealing. Incorporating trending sounds or challenges can also increase your reach, as TikTok's algorithm favors content that aligns with popular trends. Furthermore, paying attention to video analytics will provide insights into what resonates with your audience, allowing you to refine your storytelling approach over time. Keeping an eye on performance metrics is crucial for understanding how well your stories are performing and where improvements can be made.

Finally, collaboration with other creators can enrich your TikTok stories and expand your audience reach. Engaging with fellow influencers or businesses in your niche can lead to innovative content ideas and cross-promotion opportunities. This networking can enhance your storytelling by introducing new perspectives and styles, making your content more dynamic and appealing. By structuring your TikTok stories thoughtfully and creatively, you can create engaging narratives that not only capture attention but also drive growth, conversions, and a lasting impact on your audience.

Incorporating Emotional Appeals

Incorporating emotional appeals into your TikTok content can significantly enhance viewer engagement and drive a more profound connection with your audience. Emotions are powerful motivators that can influence viewer behavior, encouraging them to share, comment, and interact with your videos. By tapping into feelings such as joy, nostalgia, or even humor, creators can craft messages that resonate on a personal level, making them more relatable and memorable. This subchapter will explore strategies for effectively weaving emotional appeals into your TikTok marketing efforts.

One effective way to evoke emotion is through storytelling. Engaging narratives allow viewers to connect with your content and see themselves in the situation you present. Whether you share a personal story about your entrepreneurial journey, the challenges you faced while starting a small business, or your experience with a viral dance challenge, these narratives can evoke empathy and inspire your audience. Use your storytelling to highlight relatable struggles and triumphs, creating a bridge between your experiences and those of your viewers.

Visual elements also play a crucial role in emotional storytelling on TikTok. The platform's dynamic video capabilities enable creators to use imagery, music, and editing techniques to amplify emotional messages. For instance, choosing the right background music can enhance the mood of your content, while visual transitions can emphasize key moments in your story. By combining compelling visuals with authentic narratives, you can create an emotional experience that encourages viewers to engage and share your content with others.

In addition to storytelling and visuals, consider leveraging humor to create emotional connections. Humor can break down barriers and make your content more approachable, allowing viewers to feel comfortable engaging with your brand. Whether you're participating in a trending dance challenge or creating a comedic skit about the ups and downs of TikTok fame, humor can create a sense of community among your audience. Furthermore, humorous content often encourages sharing, expanding your reach and visibility on the platform.

Finally, it's essential to remain authentic when incorporating emotional appeals. Audiences can quickly detect insincerity, which can lead to disengagement or mistrust. When crafting emotional content, ensure that it aligns with your brand identity and values. Authenticity fosters trust and loyalty, encouraging viewers to return to your content and share it within their networks. By striking a balance between emotional resonance and genuine expression, you can enhance your TikTok marketing strategy and build a lasting impact on your audience.

Chapter 9: TikTok Video Editing Tips and Tools

Essential Editing Tools for TikTok

When creating content for TikTok, having the right editing tools can significantly elevate the quality of your videos. The platform thrives on creativity, and with the right tools, you can enhance your storytelling, dance challenges, or marketing messages to resonate better with your audience. Essential editing tools can range from user-friendly apps to software that offers advanced features, catering to various skill levels and content needs.

One of the most popular and accessible editing tools for TikTok creators is CapCut. This app is particularly favored for its intuitive interface and robust features. Users can trim clips, add music, apply filters, and incorporate text overlays seamlessly. CapCut also includes effects that can make your videos stand out, whether you're participating in viral challenges or showcasing products for your small business. Its compatibility with TikTok makes it an ideal choice for content creators looking to streamline their workflow.

For those who want to explore more advanced editing capabilities, Adobe Premiere Rush is a powerful option. This software provides a professional-grade editing experience while still being user-friendly. Adobe Premiere Rush allows creators to edit video, audio, and graphics in one platform. It is especially beneficial for influencers focused on brand collaborations, as it offers tools for color correction and audio enhancements, ensuring your content looks polished and engaging when pursuing sponsorships or affiliate marketing opportunities.

In addition to video editing tools, leveraging sound editing apps like InShot can elevate your TikTok content. This app allows you to manage audio tracks, voiceovers, and sound effects, giving your videos an additional layer of professionalism. For creators involved in storytelling or those who prioritize audio in their content, InShot can help ensure that the sound quality matches the visual appeal, making for a more immersive viewer experience.

Finally, analytics tools such as TikTok Analytics or third-party apps like Hootsuite can provide valuable insights into your content's performance. Understanding metrics like views, engagement rates, and audience demographics is crucial for tailoring your content strategy. By analyzing what works and what doesn't, you can refine your approach to reach your target audience more effectively, whether you're focusing on niche-specific growth hacks or broadening your personal brand on the platform. With the right combination of editing and analytics tools, you can maximize your impact on TikTok and drive your success in this dynamic space.

Tips for Captivating Edits

Captivating edits are essential for standing out on TikTok, where content is abundant and attention spans are short. To create edits that catch the eye, start with a clear vision of your message or story. Each clip should contribute to the narrative, whether you're promoting a product or showcasing a dance challenge. Plan your shots carefully, considering how they flow together to maintain viewer engagement. A well-thought-out sequence keeps your audience invested, encouraging them to watch until the end and interact with your content.

The use of music and sound effects can significantly enhance your edits. TikTok thrives on audio, so selecting the right soundtrack can elevate your video from ordinary to extraordinary. Syncing your cuts to the beat of the music not only makes your video more enjoyable but also creates a sense of rhythm that draws viewers in. Additionally, using trending sounds can increase your visibility, as users often search for videos associated with specific audio clips. Experimenting with different genres and styles can help you identify what resonates best with your audience.

Transitions play a crucial role in creating seamless edits. Smooth transitions can enhance the storytelling aspect of your TikTok videos, making them feel more polished and professional. There are various techniques you can employ, such as jump cuts, fades, and creative effects that align with the theme of your video. The smoother the transition, the more likely viewers will stay engaged, as it reduces the jarring effect that can occur when switching scenes abruptly. Learning to master transitions can set your content apart from the competition.

Incorporating text and graphics can also add an engaging layer to your edits. Whether you're highlighting key points, adding humor, or providing context, well-placed text can enhance understanding and retention. Using branded colors or fonts can help reinforce your personal brand, making your videos instantly recognizable. Be mindful, however, not to overcrowd your visuals; balance is key to ensuring that your message remains clear and impactful. Tools and apps designed for TikTok editing often offer customizable templates that make this process easier.

Finally, always analyze and adjust your editing style based on audience feedback and performance metrics. TikTok provides analytics that can offer insights into what types of edits resonate most with your viewers. Pay attention to engagement rates, watch time, and audience retention to understand which elements of your edits are successful. This data-driven approach allows for continuous improvement, enabling you to refine your editing techniques and stay relevant within your niche. Being adaptable and open to change is a crucial aspect of creating captivating edits that drive influencer impact on TikTok.

Enhancing Videos with Effects and Filters

Enhancing videos with effects and filters is a crucial strategy for capturing attention on TikTok, where creativity and visual appeal play significant roles in content success. With millions of videos uploaded daily, standing out requires more than just good ideas; it necessitates the use of engaging video effects and filters that can elevate the overall production quality. TikTok offers a plethora of built-in effects, from simple color adjustments to complex augmented reality overlays, allowing creators to enhance their storytelling and make their content more appealing to viewers.

Using filters can dramatically change the mood and tone of a video. For example, a warm filter can evoke a sense of nostalgia, while a cool filter might give a modern and vibrant feel. By experimenting with different filters, creators can find the right aesthetic that aligns with their brand identity or the message they wish to convey. Additionally, the use of trending filters can help tap into current trends, increasing the chances of a video going viral. Identifying and leveraging these popular filters in timely ways can keep content fresh and relevant.

Effects, on the other hand, can add dynamic elements that engage viewers. From slow-motion to speed ramps, adding movement can enhance storytelling by emphasizing key moments within the video. For dance challenges, effects like "time freeze" or "reverse" can create fun and unexpected twists that captivate audiences. It's essential to consider the pacing and rhythm of the video when applying these effects, as they should complement the content rather than distract from it. Careful selection and application of effects can enhance user experience and boost engagement rates.

In addition to built-in options, there are numerous external editing tools available for

TikTok creators. Apps like InShot, CapCut, and Adobe Premiere Rush provide advanced editing capabilities that allow for more precise control over effects and filters. These tools enable creators to layer multiple effects, create transitions, and fine-tune their videos to achieve a professional look. Understanding how to use these tools effectively can significantly enhance video quality, making content more shareable and appealing to a wider audience.

Finally, it's vital to analyze the impact of these enhancements on audience engagement. Utilizing TikTok's analytics features, creators can track how different effects and filters influence viewer behavior, such as watch time, shares, and likes. By assessing which enhancements resonate most with their audience, creators can refine their content strategies to optimize engagement and growth. Ultimately, mastering the art of video enhancement through effects and filters is not just about aesthetics; it's about crafting a compelling narrative that resonates with viewers and strengthens a creator's presence on TikTok.

Chapter 10: Building a Personal Brand on TikTok

Establishing Your Brand Identity

Establishing your brand identity on TikTok is crucial for standing out in a crowded marketplace. With millions of users and countless creators vying for attention, defining who you are and what you represent will set the foundation for your success. Your brand identity encompasses your visual aesthetics, messaging, and the overall vibe of your content. It reflects your values, mission, and the unique perspective you bring to your niche. By clearly articulating your brand identity, you can attract a loyal audience that resonates with your content and is more likely to engage with and share it.

To start building your brand identity, consider your target audience. Understanding who you want to reach will shape your content strategy and help you create videos that appeal directly to their interests and needs. Conduct research to identify the demographics of your audience, such as age, gender, and preferences. This knowledge will guide your tone, style, and the type of content you produce. For instance, if your target audience consists of young entrepreneurs, your content might focus on motivational tips and business strategies, all while maintaining an upbeat and relatable tone.

Visual elements play a significant role in establishing your brand identity on TikTok. Consistency in colors, fonts, and imagery helps create a recognizable look that users can associate with your brand. Choose a color palette that reflects your personality and the emotions you want to evoke. Your profile picture should be clear and representative of your brand, while your videos should maintain a cohesive aesthetic. This visual consistency not only enhances brand recognition but also helps users quickly identify your content as they scroll through their feeds.

In addition to visuals, your messaging is essential for conveying your brand identity. Determine the key messages you want to communicate and ensure they align with your values and mission. Your captions, voiceovers, and even the dialogue in your videos should reflect these messages. Engaging storytelling techniques can further enhance your brand identity, allowing you to connect with your audience on a deeper level. Sharing personal experiences, challenges, and successes can humanize your brand and foster a community around your content.

Finally, engaging with your audience is a critical aspect of establishing your brand identity. Respond to comments, participate in trends, and collaborate with other creators to build rapport with your followers. This interaction not only reinforces your identity but also encourages loyalty and advocacy among your audience. By nurturing these relationships, you create a supportive community that amplifies your brand's reach, ultimately leading to greater success on TikTok. As you refine your brand identity, remember that authenticity is key; staying true to yourself will resonate more deeply with your audience and help you achieve lasting impact.

Consistency in Content and Messaging

Consistency in content and messaging is a cornerstone of successful TikTok marketing. In a platform where trends shift rapidly, maintaining a coherent identity helps creators and brands stand out. Consistent messaging not only reinforces brand recognition but also fosters trust among followers. When viewers can identify a creator's voice, style, and thematic focus, they are more likely to engage with the content, share it, and become loyal fans. This consistency should extend across all aspects of content, including visual elements, tone of voice, and the overall message.

For small businesses, establishing a consistent presence on TikTok means aligning content with the brand's core values and mission. This involves creating videos that reflect the brand's personality while also catering to the TikTok culture. Small businesses should aim to tell stories that resonate with their target audience, using familiar formats and styles that viewers expect. Whether it's through humor, information, or showcasing products, a consistent approach helps reinforce the brand's identity and makes it easier for potential customers to connect with the business.

In the realm of viral dance challenges and trends, consistency doesn't mean sticking to a single type of content. Instead, it involves a strategic approach to participating in trends that fit the brand's narrative. For influencers engaging in viral challenges, it's essential to find ways to incorporate personal branding into the trend while maintaining the integrity of the challenge itself. This balance allows creators to remain relevant within the broader TikTok landscape while still promoting their unique identity, thus enhancing their visibility and engagement.

For those focused on analytics and performance tracking, consistency is also vital in evaluating what works and what doesn't. By regularly analyzing viewer engagement metrics alongside content output, creators can identify patterns that inform future content strategies. This data-driven approach ensures that messaging remains aligned with audience expectations, ultimately leading to improved performance over time. By maintaining a steady output of content that reflects both the findings from analytics and the creator's established brand, success on TikTok becomes a more achievable goal.

Building a personal brand on TikTok requires a deliberate effort to maintain consistency in messaging across collaborations and networking. As influencers partner with other creators or brands, it's crucial to ensure that any joint content aligns with their established brand identity. This consistency not only enhances credibility but also attracts followers who appreciate authenticity. Ultimately, a well-defined and consistent messaging strategy paves the way for monetization opportunities, such as sponsorships and affiliate marketing, as brands are more likely to engage with creators who present a cohesive and trustworthy image.

Engaging with Your Audience

Engaging with your audience on TikTok is crucial for building a loyal following and ensuring your content resonates. Understanding your audience's preferences, behaviors, and demographics is the starting point for effective engagement. Utilize TikTok's analytics tools to gather insights about who is watching your videos, what times they are most active, and which content types drive the most interaction. This data will guide your content creation process, allowing you to tailor your videos to meet the interests and expectations of your target audience.

Creating authentic connections with your viewers is vital for fostering engagement. Responding to comments and messages, asking questions in your videos, and encouraging viewers to share their thoughts can help create a community around your content. Consider incorporating user-generated content or challenges into your strategy, which not only encourages interaction but also makes your audience feel valued and included. This collaborative approach can drive organic growth, as viewers are more likely to share content that features their contributions.

Another effective way to engage with your audience is through storytelling. TikTok thrives on creative narratives, and using storytelling techniques can captivate your viewers and keep them coming back for more. Whether you are sharing personal experiences, showcasing customer testimonials, or framing your content around a relatable scenario, a good story can forge emotional connections. Be sure to keep your stories concise and visually engaging to maintain viewer interest in the fast-paced environment of TikTok.

Utilizing trends and challenges is another powerful method for audience engagement. Participating in viral dance challenges or trending hashtags not only increases your visibility but also invites viewers to interact with your content. When you take part in these trends, consider putting your unique spin on them to stand out. This creativity can spark conversations, encourage shares, and elevate your status within the TikTok community, ultimately driving more traffic to your profile.

Finally, collaboration is a key strategy for engaging with your audience on TikTok. Partnering with other creators or brands can introduce your content to new viewers and foster a sense of community. Whether it's co-creating videos, hosting joint live sessions, or simply shouting each other out, collaborations can amplify your reach and enhance engagement. As you network with other influencers, remember to maintain authenticity in these partnerships, ensuring that your collaborations align with your personal brand and resonate with your audience.

Chapter 11: TikTok Collaborations and Networking

Finding the Right Collaboration Partners

Finding the right collaboration partners on TikTok is crucial for maximizing your content's reach and effectiveness. In a platform where trends shift rapidly, aligning with the right individuals or brands can elevate your account and help you tap into new audiences. Begin by identifying your niche and understanding what kind of collaborations will resonate with your followers. Consider factors such as the partner's follower count, engagement rate, and overall content style. A partner with a similar audience demographic can enhance your visibility and credibility, making it easier to build authentic connections with viewers.

Once you have a clear understanding of your niche, start exploring potential partners. Look for influencers or businesses who are already active in your space. This can include those who participate in viral dance challenges, engage in storytelling techniques, or utilize specific marketing strategies. Use TikTok's search function, hashtags, and trends to discover creators who align with your brand values and content goals. Engaging with their content by liking, commenting, and sharing can also help establish rapport before proposing a collaboration.

When approaching potential partners, be clear about what you hope to achieve through the collaboration. Craft a compelling pitch that outlines the mutual benefits, whether it be increased exposure, shared resources, or enhanced content quality. Highlight how the collaboration will provide value to both parties and their respective audiences. A well-thought-out proposal can make a significant difference, showing that you are serious and professional about the partnership.

Moreover, consider the dynamics of the collaboration. Whether you're planning a joint video, a challenge, or a live event, it's essential to maintain open communication throughout the process. Discuss creative ideas, timelines, and expectations to ensure that both parties are on the same page. Flexibility and collaboration can lead to innovative content that showcases the strengths of both creators. The more seamless the partnership feels, the more genuine the content will appear to your audience.

Lastly, after executing the collaboration, evaluate its success through analytics and performance tracking. Analyze engagement metrics such as views, likes, shares, and comments to determine what worked well and what can be improved for future collaborations. This data not only helps refine your strategy but also provides insights into your audience's preferences. By continuously seeking the right partners and optimizing your collaborative efforts, you can enhance your TikTok presence and drive growth for your brand or business.

Strategies for Successful Collaborations

Successful collaborations on TikTok can significantly enhance your reach and impact, making it crucial to understand effective strategies for partnering with others. One of the first steps in establishing a fruitful collaboration is identifying partners who align with your brand values and audience. This alignment ensures that the content resonates with both parties' followers, fostering a more genuine connection. Whether you are a small business looking to expand your reach or an influencer aiming to diversify your content, finding collaborators who share a similar niche can amplify your message and create a more engaging experience.

Once you've identified potential collaborators, it's essential to communicate openly about your goals and expectations. Discussing the type of content you want to create together, the target audience, and the desired outcomes can help streamline the creative process. Establishing clear roles and responsibilities can also prevent misunderstandings and ensure that both parties are invested in the collaboration's success. Utilizing shared documents or project management tools can aid in keeping track of ideas, deadlines, and responsibilities, which is particularly useful when working with multiple collaborators.

Creativity is at the heart of successful TikTok collaborations. To stand out in a crowded space, consider brainstorming unique concepts that blend both partners' styles and strengths. This could involve combining viral dance challenges with storytelling elements or creating a series that addresses niche-specific topics. Engaging content often results from taking risks and experimenting with new formats. Encouraging open feedback during the creative process can lead to innovative ideas that capture the attention of your target audience and drive engagement.

Promoting the collaboration effectively is key to maximizing its impact. Utilize both partners' platforms to share the content and engage with followers, creating excitement around the collaboration. Cross-promotional strategies, such as shoutouts, behind-the-scenes previews, or interactive Q&A sessions, can build anticipation and encourage more views. Additionally, leveraging TikTok's features, such as duets and stitches, can enhance engagement and encourage the community to participate in the trends you create together.

Finally, analyzing the performance of your collaboration is vital for understanding its effectiveness and making improvements in future partnerships. Utilize TikTok analytics to track engagement metrics such as views, likes, shares, and comments. This data can provide insights into what worked well and what didn't, allowing you to refine your approach for future collaborations. Sharing these insights with your partner can foster a learning environment, creating a foundation for even more successful collaborations down the line. By adopting these strategies, you can ensure that your TikTok collaborations are not only successful but also enjoyable and rewarding for all involved.

Building a Network of Influencers

Building a network of influencers is essential for anyone looking to maximize their impact on TikTok. Influencers can amplify your message, expand your audience, and create collaborative opportunities that enhance engagement. The first step in building this network is identifying influencers within your niche who align with your brand values and goals. Look for individuals who not only have a significant following but also engage authentically with their audience. Tools like TikTok's Discover page or third-party analytics platforms can help you locate potential partners.

Once you have identified potential influencers, the next step is to establish a genuine connection. Engage with their content by liking, commenting, and sharing your thoughts on their posts. This not only helps you get noticed but also allows you to understand their style and audience better. Personalize your outreach when you finally initiate contact; a thoughtful message that shows you appreciate their work and highlights mutual interests can go a long way in building a rapport. Avoid generic outreach, as it often leads to missed opportunities.

Collaboration is a powerful strategy for building your influencer network. Once you have established a connection, propose collaborative projects that can benefit both parties. These could include joint TikTok challenges, co-hosted live sessions, or even cross-promotions. Collaborating allows you to tap into each other's audiences, providing exposure to new followers who may be interested in your content. Such partnerships can also foster creativity, leading to innovative content that stands out in the crowded TikTok landscape.

As you expand your network, it's crucial to maintain these relationships. Regular communication, updates on each other's work, and continued engagement with their content can help solidify your network. Consider hosting virtual meet-ups or participating in influencer events to strengthen these connections further. Additionally, showcasing your collaborators in your content can create a sense of community and encourage reciprocal promotion, enhancing the visibility of all parties involved.

Finally, track the effectiveness of your influencer collaborations using TikTok analytics. Monitoring key performance indicators like engagement rates, follower growth, and video shares can provide insights into what strategies are working and what may need adjustment. This data-driven approach will help you refine your networking efforts, ensuring that you build a robust network of influencers that not only elevates your brand but also contributes to your long-term success on TikTok.

Chapter 12: Monetizing TikTok: Sponsorships and Affiliate Marketing

Understanding Monetization Opportunities

Understanding monetization opportunities on TikTok is essential for anyone looking to capitalize on their content creation efforts. As the platform continues to grow in popularity, it has become a lucrative avenue not only for influencers but also for small businesses and brands seeking to connect with their audience. By leveraging viral trends, engaging storytelling techniques, and innovative marketing strategies, creators can tap into various revenue streams that TikTok offers. This subchapter will explore these monetization opportunities, providing insight into how users can effectively monetize their presence on the platform.

One of the primary monetization avenues on TikTok is through sponsorships. Brands are increasingly turning to influencers to promote their products and services, recognizing the platform's unique ability to reach a diverse audience. Influencers can collaborate with companies to create authentic content that aligns with their personal brand and resonates with their followers. This partnership not only provides financial compensation but also enhances the influencer's credibility and visibility within their niche. Understanding how to pitch to brands and negotiate deals is crucial for maximizing these opportunities.

Affiliate marketing is another effective way to monetize TikTok content. By sharing unique affiliate links in their profiles or video descriptions, creators can earn commissions on sales generated through their referrals. This approach works well for both influencers and small businesses, as it allows them to promote products they genuinely believe in while earning passive income. Creators should focus on building a trustworthy relationship with their audience, as authenticity is key to successful affiliate marketing. By consistently delivering valuable content and promoting relevant products, influencers can drive engagement and conversions.

Beyond sponsorships and affiliate marketing, TikTok also offers creators the chance to earn money directly through the platform's Creator Fund. This program compensates users based on the performance of their videos, providing an additional revenue stream for those who produce high-quality and engaging content. To qualify, creators must meet specific criteria, including follower count and video views. Understanding TikTok analytics and performance tracking is vital for creators to optimize their content strategy and increase their chances of earning through the Creator Fund.

Lastly, collaborations and networking within the TikTok community can lead to new monetization opportunities. By partnering with other creators, influencers can expand their reach and tap into different audiences. These collaborations can take many forms, from joint challenges and dance videos to co-hosted live sessions. Building a personal brand that emphasizes collaboration not only enhances visibility but also opens doors to potential sponsorship deals and partnerships. By understanding the importance of community and leveraging relationships, TikTok users can create a sustainable and profitable presence on the platform.

Approaching Brands for Sponsorships

Approaching brands for sponsorships requires a strategic mindset and a clear understanding of what both parties can gain from the partnership. Before reaching out to potential sponsors, it's essential to identify brands that resonate with your content and audience on TikTok. Research brands that align with your niche, whether it's dance, storytelling, or small business promotion. Consider their previous collaborations and marketing campaigns to gauge how your partnership might fit within their overall strategy. This targeted approach increases the likelihood of securing sponsorships that are genuine and beneficial.

Once you have a list of potential brands, it's time to craft a compelling pitch. Your pitch should highlight your unique value proposition as an influencer and how your audience aligns with the brand's target demographic. Include specific metrics from your TikTok analytics, such as follower count, engagement rates, and past campaign successes. This data serves as evidence of your influence and the potential return on investment for the brand. Be concise yet persuasive, ensuring that your message clearly conveys why a partnership would be advantageous for both parties.

Building a relationship with brands prior to pitching can also enhance your chances of securing sponsorships. Engage with their content on TikTok and other social media platforms by liking, commenting, and sharing. This not only helps you stay informed about the brand's activities but also allows you to establish a rapport. When you eventually reach out for sponsorships, your previous interactions will make your proposal feel less transactional and more like a continuation of a conversation you've already started.

When negotiating sponsorship deals, be transparent about what you can offer. Outline the type of content you'll create, the timeline for delivery, and the specific platforms where the content will be shared. Discuss compensation openly, whether it be monetary or in the form of products and services. Understanding the brand's budget and expectations can lead to a mutually beneficial agreement. Be willing to negotiate terms that work for both you and the brand, fostering a long-term relationship rather than a one-off collaboration.

Finally, after securing a sponsorship, it's crucial to deliver high-quality content that meets or exceeds the brand's expectations. This not only solidifies your reputation as a reliable influencer but also lays the groundwork for future collaborations. Monitor the performance of your sponsored content using TikTok analytics to provide feedback to the brand. Sharing the results of your campaign can demonstrate your impact and effectiveness, making it easier to approach them for future partnerships. By approaching brands thoughtfully and professionally, you can create successful sponsorships that enhance your influence and contribute to your overall growth on TikTok.

Leveraging Affiliate Marketing on TikTok

Leveraging affiliate marketing on TikTok presents a unique opportunity for content creators and businesses alike to monetize their presence on the platform. Unlike traditional advertising methods, affiliate marketing allows individuals to promote products or services they genuinely believe in, earning a commission for each sale generated through their unique affiliate links. This approach not only fosters authenticity but also encourages creators to engage their audience meaningfully, as followers are more likely to trust recommendations that come from relatable sources.

The first step in leveraging affiliate marketing on TikTok is selecting the right products or services to promote. Creators should focus on items that align with their personal brand and resonate with their audience. For example, a beauty influencer might promote skincare products, while a fitness enthusiast could share workout gear or nutritional supplements. By ensuring that the promoted products are relevant to their niche, creators can enhance their credibility and increase the likelihood of conversions. Additionally, it's essential to choose affiliate programs that offer competitive commissions and reliable tracking systems to monitor performance.

Once the right products are selected, creators need to craft engaging content that showcases these items effectively. TikTok's short-form video format encourages creativity, and influencers can utilize trends, challenges, and storytelling techniques to highlight the benefits of the products they are promoting. For instance, a creator could participate in a viral dance challenge while using a sponsored product, seamlessly integrating the promotion into the entertaining content. This approach not only captivates viewers but also provides an organic way to introduce affiliate links without coming off as overly sales-focused.

To maximize the reach of affiliate marketing efforts, creators should employ strategic hashtags and trends to enhance discoverability. Utilizing niche-specific hashtags can help target a more relevant audience, while participating in trending challenges can attract new followers who may be interested in the promoted products. Moreover, creators should engage with their audience through comments and direct messages, fostering a community that trusts their recommendations. Building this rapport is crucial for driving conversions, as followers are more likely to purchase products recommended by creators they feel connected to.

Finally, tracking performance and analyzing TikTok analytics is vital for optimizing affiliate marketing strategies. Creators should monitor metrics such as views, engagement rates, and conversion rates to assess which types of content resonate best with their audience. This data-driven approach allows for continuous improvement and refinement of marketing tactics. By understanding what works and what doesn't, creators can adapt their strategies to enhance their affiliate marketing efforts, ultimately driving more sales and increasing their revenue on TikTok.

www.ingramcontent.com/pod-product-compliance
Lightning Source LLC
Chambersburg PA
CBHW071004050326
40689CB00014B/3483